Building a Strong Foundation: The Power of Value Education in Character Development

Anthony

Copyright © [2023]

Title: Building a Strong Foundation: The Power of Value Education in Character Development

Author's: Anthony

All rights reserved. No part of this publication may be reproduced, stored in a retrieval system, or transmitted in any form or by any means, electronic, mechanical, photocopying, recording, or otherwise, without the prior written permission of the publisher or author, except in the case of brief quotations embodied in critical reviews and certain other non-commercial uses permitted by copyright law.

This book was printed and published by [Publisher's: **Anthony**] in [2023]

ISBN:

TABLE OF CONTENT

Chapter 1: Understanding Value Education 07

Defining Value Education

The Importance of Value Education in Character Development

Chapter 2: Core Values for Character Development 11

Respect and Empathy

Responsibility and Accountability

Integrity and Honesty

Compassion and Kindness

Perseverance and Resilience

Chapter 3: Implementing Value Education in Schools 21

Integrating Value Education into the Curriculum

Creating a Positive Learning Environment

Teacher's Role in Value Education

Parental Involvement in Reinforcing Values

Chapter 4: Teaching Methods for Value Education 29

Storytelling and Role-Playing

Group Discussions and Debates

Case Studies and Real-Life Examples

Service-Learning Projects

Reflection and Self-Assessment

Chapter 5: Assessing Character Development through Value Education 39

Evaluating Character Traits

Self-Reflection and Self-Assessment Tools

Feedback and Support for Continuous Growth

## Chapter 6: Addressing Challenges in Value Education	45

Overcoming Resistance to Change

Dealing with Diverse Value Systems

Handling Ethical Dilemmas

## Chapter 7: The Role of Value Education in Building a Strong Society	51

Building Ethical Leaders

Promoting Social Responsibility

Fostering Inclusive and Harmonious Communities

## Chapter 8: The Long-Term Impact of Value Education on Students	57

Enhancing Emotional Intelligence and Interpersonal Skills

Developing a Strong Moral Compass

Nurturing Ethical Decision-Making Skills

Chapter 9: Value Education Beyond the Classroom 63

Community Engagement and Volunteerism

Applying Values in Real-Life Situations

Creating a Lasting Legacy

Chapter 10: Conclusion and Future of Value Education 69

Recap of Key Learnings

Embracing Value Education for a Better Future

Chapter 1: Understanding Value Education

Defining Value Education

In today's fast-paced and competitive world, where success is often measured solely by material accomplishments and academic achievements, the importance of value education cannot be overstated. While academic knowledge is undoubtedly crucial, it is equally important to cultivate a strong moral compass, empathy, and integrity. Building a Strong Foundation: The Power of Value Education in Character Development aims to explore the significance of value education, not only for students but for everyone.

Value education refers to the process of inculcating ethical values, social skills, and character development in individuals. It goes beyond the traditional classroom curriculum, seeking to instill qualities such as honesty, compassion, respect, responsibility, and tolerance. By integrating these values into our daily lives, we can contribute positively to society and lead fulfilling lives.

For students, value education plays a pivotal role in shaping their character and overall development. It equips them with essential life skills that go beyond academics, enabling them to navigate challenges, make ethical decisions, and build meaningful relationships. Students who receive value education are more likely to exhibit strong leadership qualities, empathy towards others, and a heightened sense of social responsibility.

However, the importance of value education extends far beyond the student population. It is equally relevant for every individual, regardless of age or occupation. In a world plagued by conflicts, inequality, and intolerance, value education offers a ray of hope. It encourages individuals to become better versions of themselves, fostering harmonious coexistence and a sense of unity among diverse communities.

Value education also serves as a compass in making important life choices. It provides clarity in decision-making processes and helps individuals distinguish between right and wrong. Moreover, value education empowers individuals to withstand societal pressures and temptations, enabling them to stay true to their beliefs and principles.

In conclusion, value education is of utmost importance for students and everyone else. It shapes character, enhances personal growth, and fosters a sense of responsibility towards society. By embracing value education, we can build a strong foundation for a better future, where integrity, compassion, and respect reign supreme. Whether you are a student embarking on your educational journey or an individual seeking personal growth, value education is the key to unlocking your full potential and making a positive impact on the world around you.

The Importance of Value Education in Character Development

In today's fast-paced and competitive world, it is essential for students and everyone to recognize the significance of value education in character development. Building a Strong Foundation: The Power of Value Education in Character Development is a book that aims to highlight the importance of value education and its impact on shaping individuals' characters.

Value education refers to the process of imparting moral and ethical values to individuals, enabling them to make responsible choices and become compassionate members of society. It goes beyond traditional academic learning and focuses on nurturing essential qualities such as empathy, integrity, respect, and self-discipline. These values form the bedrock of an individual's character and play a vital role in shaping their actions, behaviors, and overall personality.

One of the key reasons why value education is so crucial is its ability to instill a sense of purpose and meaning in individuals' lives. By understanding and internalizing values, students can develop a strong moral compass that guides them in making ethical decisions. They become aware of the consequences of their actions and learn to prioritize honesty, fairness, and empathy in their interactions with others.

Furthermore, value education equips individuals with essential life skills that are not typically taught in traditional academic curricula. It empowers them to develop critical thinking abilities, problem-solving skills, and effective communication techniques. These skills are essential for success in various aspects of life, including personal relationships, professional endeavors, and social interactions.

Moreover, value education plays a significant role in fostering a positive and inclusive school environment. Students who receive value education are more likely to exhibit respect for diversity, kindness, and tolerance towards others. They become active contributors to their communities, striving to create a harmonious and inclusive society.

In conclusion, the importance of value education in character development cannot be overstated. Building a Strong Foundation: The Power of Value Education in Character Development emphasizes the transformative role of value education in nurturing individuals' characters and shaping their lives. By instilling moral and ethical values, value education equips students with the necessary tools to become responsible, compassionate, and successful individuals in all spheres of life.

Chapter 2: Core Values for Character Development

Respect and Empathy

Respect and Empathy: The Cornerstones of Character Development

In our fast-paced and interconnected world, it is easy to get caught up in our own lives and forget about the importance of respect and empathy. However, these two values are the essential building blocks of character development, and they hold immense power in shaping a strong foundation for our personal growth and relationships.

Respect, at its core, is about recognizing the inherent worth and dignity of every individual. It goes beyond mere politeness and extends to listening attentively, acknowledging different perspectives, and treating others with kindness and fairness. By practicing respect, we create an inclusive and harmonious environment where everyone feels valued and appreciated.

Empathy, on the other hand, is the ability to understand and share the feelings of others. It allows us to step into someone else's shoes and view the world from their perspective. Through empathy, we develop a deeper sense of connection with those around us and foster meaningful relationships built on understanding and compassion.

As students, understanding the importance of respect and empathy is crucial for our personal and academic growth. In the classroom, it is essential to respect our teachers, peers, and their ideas. By valuing their contributions and embracing diversity, we create an environment that encourages learning, collaboration, and innovation.

Respect and empathy also play a vital role in building strong relationships beyond the classroom. Whether it is our family, friends, or colleagues, treating others with respect and empathy strengthens the bonds of trust and fosters a supportive network. These qualities are particularly important in resolving conflicts and finding common ground, as they promote open dialogue and compromise.

Moreover, the significance of respect and empathy extends beyond our immediate circles. In a diverse society, understanding and appreciating different cultures, beliefs, and backgrounds is key to promoting tolerance and peaceful coexistence. By practicing respect and empathy towards others, we contribute to creating a world where everyone feels valued, understood, and accepted.

In conclusion, respect and empathy are not only essential values in character development but also fundamental components of a harmonious and inclusive society. As students, it is crucial for us to embrace these values and practice them in our daily lives. By doing so, we lay the groundwork for personal growth, meaningful relationships, and a better world for all. Let us remember that respect and empathy are not signs of weakness but rather strengths that empower us to build a strong foundation for a brighter future.

Responsibility and Accountability

In today's fast-paced and interconnected world, it is more important than ever for individuals to understand the significance of responsibility and accountability. These two values form the bedrock of a strong foundation in character development. In this subchapter, we will explore the importance of responsibility and accountability in our lives and how they are tied to the power of value education.

Responsibility can be defined as the state or fact of having a duty to deal with something or someone, while accountability refers to the willingness to accept responsibility for one's actions and decisions. These values are not only vital for personal growth but also for the betterment of society as a whole.

For students, understanding and embracing responsibility is crucial in achieving success academically and in their future careers. It means taking ownership of their actions and choices, whether it be completing assignments on time or studying diligently. By being responsible, students develop a sense of self-discipline and resilience, enabling them to face challenges and overcome obstacles.

Accountability, on the other hand, plays a pivotal role in fostering trust and reliability. It is about being answerable for one's behavior and acknowledging the consequences of one's actions. When individuals are accountable, they become more trustworthy and dependable, qualities that are highly valued in personal and professional relationships.

Value education, with its focus on instilling moral and ethical principles, provides a solid framework for understanding responsibility and accountability. By emphasizing the importance of integrity, empathy, and respect, value education helps individuals develop a sense of duty towards themselves and others. It teaches students to make conscious choices that align with their values and to take responsibility for their actions.

In conclusion, responsibility and accountability are essential values in character development. They empower individuals to take charge of their lives, make ethical decisions, and contribute positively to society. Value education serves as a catalyst for instilling these values in students, helping them build a strong foundation for personal and professional success. By embracing responsibility and accountability, students and everyone can become agents of positive change in the world.

Integrity and Honesty

In a world where values are often compromised, understanding the importance of integrity and honesty is crucial for both students and everyone else. This subchapter aims to shed light on these essential virtues and their significance in character development. By emphasizing the power of value education, we can build a strong foundation for a better future.

Integrity is the quality of being honest and having strong moral principles. It involves doing the right thing, even when no one is watching. Honesty, on the other hand, is the act of truthfulness and transparency. These values go hand in hand, forming the backbone of our character and guiding our actions.

For students, integrity and honesty are vital for personal growth and success. Upholding these virtues allows you to develop a strong sense of self, gain the respect and trust of others, and establish a positive reputation. By consistently acting with integrity, you demonstrate your commitment to your values and show that you can be relied upon.

In every aspect of life, be it academics, relationships, or professional endeavors, integrity and honesty play a crucial role. They contribute to an environment of trust and foster healthy interactions, ensuring that everyone is treated fairly. Employers, for instance, highly value individuals with integrity, as they can be entrusted with responsibilities and are more likely to adhere to ethical standards.

The importance of value education cannot be underestimated in cultivating integrity and honesty. It equips individuals with the knowledge and skills to make ethical decisions and take responsibility for their actions. Through value education, students learn to differentiate between right and wrong, understand the consequences of their choices, and develop a strong moral compass.

Furthermore, value education helps students develop empathy and compassion, enabling them to understand the impact of their actions on others. By instilling a sense of integrity from an early age, we can raise a generation of individuals who value honesty and act with integrity in all aspects of their lives.

In conclusion, integrity and honesty are fundamental values that should be instilled in students and embraced by everyone. By recognizing the importance of value education, we can lay the groundwork for character development and create a society built on trust, fairness, and accountability. Let us strive to uphold these virtues, both in our personal lives and in our interactions with others, to build a strong foundation for a brighter future.

Compassion and Kindness

Compassion and Kindness: The Pillars of a Strong Foundation

In this fast-paced world, where competition and individual success often take center stage, it is easy to overlook the importance of compassion and kindness in our daily lives. However, the truth is that these virtues are not only essential for building strong character but also for creating a harmonious and empathetic society. In this subchapter, we will explore the significance of compassion and kindness in value education, and how they contribute to the overall development of individuals.

Compassion, at its core, is the ability to understand and share the feelings of others. It is the driving force behind acts of kindness and empathy, allowing us to connect with those around us on a deeper level. By cultivating compassion, students can develop a heightened sense of awareness towards the struggles and challenges faced by their peers, fostering a supportive and inclusive environment within their educational communities.

Kindness, on the other hand, is the expression of compassion through actions. Small acts of kindness can have a profound impact not only on the recipient but also on the giver. Whether it is offering a helping hand to a struggling classmate or simply smiling at someone who looks down, acts of kindness create a ripple effect of positivity that can transform the atmosphere of any setting. By practicing kindness, students can not only improve their own well-being but also inspire others to do the same.

The importance of value education in instilling compassion and kindness cannot be overstated. While academic achievements are undeniably important, it is the cultivation of these virtues that truly molds individuals into well-rounded and empathetic beings. By incorporating value education into the curriculum, students are provided with a platform to explore their own values and beliefs, and to understand the impact of their actions on others.

Furthermore, the benefits of compassion and kindness extend far beyond the individual level. In a world plagued by conflict and division, these virtues have the power to bridge gaps and foster understanding among diverse communities. By equipping students with the tools to practice compassion and kindness, we are laying the foundation for a more compassionate and harmonious society.

In conclusion, compassion and kindness are not just idealistic concepts; they are essential values that should be fostered and nurtured in every individual. By integrating value education into our curriculum, we can empower students to become compassionate and kind individuals, capable of making a positive impact on the world around them. Let us embrace these values and steer our society towards a future filled with empathy, understanding, and unity.

Perseverance and Resilience

In the journey of life, we often face numerous challenges, obstacles, and setbacks. It is during these moments that the virtues of perseverance and resilience become crucial. Perseverance is the ability to keep going, to never give up, even when the going gets tough. Resilience, on the other hand, is the capacity to bounce back from adversity, to overcome setbacks, and to emerge stronger than before. These two virtues form the backbone of character development and are essential for success in any endeavor.

For students and everyone alike, the importance of value education cannot be overstated. It is through value education that we learn about the significance of perseverance and resilience, and how they can shape our lives for the better. Value education teaches us the power of determination, motivating us to push through challenges and keep striving towards our goals, no matter how difficult the path may seem.

Perseverance is the fuel that propels us forward, even when we face seemingly insurmountable obstacles. It is the mindset that enables us to turn setbacks into stepping stones, to learn from failures, and to keep moving towards our dreams. When we persevere, we develop mental strength and resilience, allowing us to face challenges head-on and come out stronger on the other side.

Resilience, on the other hand, is the armor that protects us from the blows of life. It is the ability to adapt to change, to bounce back from failure, and to embrace challenges as opportunities for growth. Resilience enables us to maintain a positive mindset, even in the face of adversity, and to keep moving forward despite setbacks. It teaches us that failure is not the end, but rather a stepping stone towards success.

Through value education, we understand that perseverance and resilience are not innate qualities, but rather skills that can be cultivated and strengthened. We learn that setbacks and failures are not roadblocks, but rather opportunities for growth and self-improvement. By embracing perseverance and resilience, we develop the mental fortitude and determination to overcome any obstacle that comes our way.

In conclusion, the subchapter of "Perseverance and Resilience" highlights the importance of value education in building a strong foundation for character development. It emphasizes the significance of perseverance and resilience in facing life's challenges and achieving success. By instilling these virtues in students and everyone, value education equips individuals with the tools necessary to overcome obstacles, bounce back from failures, and ultimately lead fulfilling and successful lives.

Chapter 3: Implementing Value Education in Schools

Integrating Value Education into the Curriculum

In today's fast-paced and competitive world, education goes beyond gaining knowledge and skills in various subjects. It is crucial to develop a strong foundation of values that will guide students throughout their lives. This subchapter explores the importance of value education and how it can be effectively integrated into the curriculum.

Value education is the process of imparting essential life values such as honesty, respect, empathy, and responsibility to students. It plays a significant role in character development and prepares individuals to become responsible citizens of society. While academic excellence is important, it is equally vital to instill values that will help students navigate challenges and make ethical decisions.

Integrating value education into the curriculum ensures that these values are not just taught as standalone lessons but are woven into various subjects and activities. By doing so, students learn to apply values in real-life situations and understand their practical significance. For example, when studying history, students can learn about the importance of honesty through stories of great leaders who displayed integrity during challenging times.

One of the key benefits of integrating value education is the holistic development of students. It helps them cultivate essential life skills such as critical thinking, problem-solving, empathy, and teamwork.

These skills are highly sought after in the professional world and contribute to personal growth as well.

Moreover, value education enhances overall well-being and mental health. By learning about values like compassion and gratitude, students develop a positive mindset and learn to appreciate the world around them. This, in turn, leads to improved self-esteem and a greater sense of purpose.

To effectively integrate value education, educators should adopt a multidimensional approach. This includes creating a safe and inclusive learning environment, incorporating value-based discussions and activities into lessons, and setting positive examples through their own behavior. Additionally, collaboration with parents and the community can reinforce the values taught in school, providing a consistent message to students.

In conclusion, the integration of value education into the curriculum is of utmost importance for students and everyone in society. By focusing not only on academic achievements but also on character development, we can build a strong foundation for future generations. Value education equips individuals with the necessary skills and values to lead meaningful lives and contribute positively to society.

Creating a Positive Learning Environment

In today's fast-paced world, education goes beyond simply acquiring knowledge and passing exams. It is about building a strong foundation for character development and personal growth. One of the key aspects of this process is creating a positive learning environment. Whether you are a student or someone interested in the importance of value education, understanding the significance of a positive learning environment is crucial.

A positive learning environment nurtures students' overall development, not just academically but also emotionally and socially. It fosters a sense of belonging, trust, and respect among students, teachers, and the entire school community. When students feel safe and supported, they are more likely to engage actively in their learning journey, leading to improved academic performance and a positive attitude towards education.

So, how can we create such an environment? Firstly, it starts with the teachers. They play a vital role in setting the tone for the classroom. By demonstrating patience, empathy, and understanding, teachers can create a safe space where students feel comfortable expressing their thoughts and ideas freely. Encouraging open communication and active participation enhances the learning experience and promotes a positive classroom atmosphere.

Another crucial element is the promotion of inclusivity. Diversity should be celebrated and respected in all aspects of education. Creating an inclusive environment means recognizing and appreciating individual differences, whether it be cultural, religious, or personal. Embracing diversity not only enriches the learning experience but also fosters empathy, tolerance, and understanding among students.

Building positive relationships among students is equally important. Encouraging teamwork, collaboration, and peer support enhances social skills and empathy. Students learn from one another's strengths and weaknesses, cultivating a sense of camaraderie and understanding. Such relationships extend beyond the classroom, contributing to a positive school culture that values cooperation and mutual respect.

Lastly, it is vital to create an environment that promotes personal growth and self-reflection. Encouraging students to set goals, celebrate achievements, and learn from failures helps them develop a growth mindset. Providing opportunities for self-expression, creativity, and independent thinking allows students to explore their potential and develop a sense of ownership over their education.

In conclusion, creating a positive learning environment is essential for students' holistic development and the cultivation of strong values. By fostering a sense of belonging, promoting inclusivity, building positive relationships, and encouraging personal growth, we can lay the foundation for a successful educational journey. Remember, a positive learning environment is not only beneficial for students but also for everyone involved in the education process.

Teacher's Role in Value Education

In the journey of life, education plays a pivotal role in shaping our character and molding us into responsible individuals. However, education is not solely about acquiring knowledge; it is also about imbibing values that guide our actions and decisions. Value education, therefore, holds significant importance in building a strong foundation for character development. And at the heart of this process lies the role of teachers.

Teachers are not just bearers of academic knowledge; they are also torchbearers of values. They are the guiding light that illuminates the path of their students, leading them towards ethical behavior, empathy, and a sense of social responsibility. A teacher's role in value education is, therefore, crucial and cannot be undermined.

First and foremost, teachers serve as role models for their students. Children observe and imitate their teachers' behavior, attitudes, and values. It is through this observance that students learn important life lessons. The values a teacher upholds in the classroom and in their personal lives greatly influence the values their students embrace. A teacher who consistently exhibits honesty, integrity, and respect will encourage their students to do the same.

Furthermore, teachers facilitate the transmission of values through their teaching methods and curriculum choices. They infuse value-based lessons into their subjects, ensuring that students understand the importance of compassion, tolerance, and cooperation. By incorporating real-life examples and engaging activities, teachers bring values to life, making them more relatable and understandable for their students.

Teachers also play a pivotal role in nurturing a positive classroom environment that fosters the growth of values. They create a safe space where students feel comfortable expressing their opinions, concerns, and emotions. By encouraging open dialogue, teachers promote tolerance, acceptance, and empathy among their students. They facilitate discussions on moral dilemmas and ethical decision-making, encouraging critical thinking and the development of strong values.

In conclusion, the role of teachers in value education cannot be overstated. They are not only responsible for imparting knowledge but also for shaping the moral compass of their students. Through their own actions, curriculum choices, and classroom management, teachers inspire and guide students towards becoming compassionate, responsible, and ethical individuals. It is through the collaborative efforts of teachers, students, and the wider community that the importance of value education can be fully realized, creating a better society for all.

Parental Involvement in Reinforcing Values

In today's rapidly changing world, the role of parents in the development of their children is more important than ever. As children grow and navigate through the complexities of life, it becomes crucial for parents to actively engage in reinforcing values that will shape their character and guide them towards becoming responsible, compassionate, and ethical individuals. This subchapter aims to highlight the significance of parental involvement in value education and how it can lay a strong foundation for character development.

Parents are the primary influencers in a child's life, and their involvement in reinforcing values is essential for several reasons. Firstly, parents serve as role models. Children observe and emulate their parents' behaviors and attitudes, making it imperative for parents to exemplify the values they wish to instill in their children. By consistently demonstrating honesty, respect, empathy, and other positive values, parents can inspire their children to adopt these virtues and incorporate them into their own lives.

Furthermore, parental involvement in value education helps children understand the importance of moral principles in decision-making. By engaging in open discussions and dialogues, parents can teach their children to critically evaluate their choices and consider the ethical consequences of their actions. This process encourages children to develop a strong moral compass, enabling them to make principled decisions even when faced with challenging situations.

Moreover, parental involvement creates a nurturing and supportive environment where children feel safe to explore their values and beliefs. By actively listening to their children's thoughts and concerns, parents can provide guidance and help shape their understanding of right and wrong. This involvement helps children feel valued and respected, fostering a sense of belonging and self-confidence that allows them to develop their own set of values based on their unique experiences and perspectives.

Lastly, parental involvement in value education strengthens the parent-child bond. By actively participating in activities that promote values such as volunteering, community service, or engaging in family rituals, parents create meaningful connections with their children. These shared experiences provide opportunities for parents to reinforce the values they cherish and encourage open communication, trust, and mutual respect.

In conclusion, parental involvement in reinforcing values is of utmost importance in building a strong foundation for character development. By serving as role models, guiding decision-making processes, creating nurturing environments, and strengthening the parent-child bond, parents play a vital role in instilling positive values in their children. The power of value education lies in its ability to shape individuals who will contribute positively to society, making it essential for students and everyone to recognize the importance of parental involvement in this process.

Chapter 4: Teaching Methods for Value Education

Storytelling and Role-Playing

Storytelling and Role-Playing: Unleashing the Power of Value Education

In today's fast-paced world, where technology seems to dominate our lives, it is easy to forget the importance of value education. Students and everyone else may wonder, why should we invest our time and energy in learning about values? The answer lies in the transformative power of storytelling and role-playing, which serve as invaluable tools in character development.

Storytelling has been an integral part of human civilization since time immemorial. Through stories, we not only entertain but also pass down knowledge, wisdom, and moral lessons from one generation to the next. Stories have the remarkable ability to capture our imagination, evoke emotions, and transport us to different worlds. They allow us to explore different perspectives, understand the consequences of actions, and learn from the experiences of others.

When it comes to value education, storytelling becomes a powerful medium for instilling virtues and ethical behavior. By immersing ourselves in the stories of noble characters who face moral dilemmas and make difficult choices, we are able to internalize the values they embody. These stories provide us with role models and inspire us to develop empathy, integrity, and resilience.

Role-playing takes this process a step further. By actively participating in the enactment of stories, students and everyone else can put themselves in the shoes of the characters, allowing them to deeply understand the challenges and complexities of ethical decision-making. Role-playing encourages critical thinking, problem-solving, and collaboration, as individuals work together to navigate through various scenarios and explore different outcomes.

Moreover, storytelling and role-playing foster creativity and imagination, skills that are increasingly valuable in our ever-changing world. They encourage individuals to think beyond the confines of their own experiences and envision a better future. By engaging in these activities, students and everyone else can develop their communication skills, learn to express themselves effectively, and explore their own values and beliefs.

In conclusion, value education is not just important, but essential for building a strong foundation of character. Through the power of storytelling and role-playing, we can tap into the transformative potential of values, instilling them in ourselves and inspiring others to do the same. So, let us embrace the magic of stories, immerse ourselves in the lives of characters, and embark on a journey of self-discovery and personal growth. Together, we can create a world where values are cherished, and individuals are empowered to make a positive difference.

Group Discussions and Debates

Engaging in group discussions and debates is a crucial aspect of value education and character development. These activities provide a platform for students and everyone to express their opinions, develop critical thinking skills, and learn from one another. In this subchapter, we will explore the importance of group discussions and debates in building a strong foundation for value education.

Group discussions allow individuals to share their thoughts and ideas on various topics. By actively participating in these discussions, students can learn to respect different viewpoints and develop empathy towards others. They learn to listen attentively and understand diverse perspectives, fostering open-mindedness and tolerance. Moreover, group discussions encourage collaboration and teamwork, as participants work together to find common ground and reach a consensus.

Debates, on the other hand, provide an intellectual arena for individuals to present arguments and counterarguments on a particular topic. Through debates, students can enhance their research and analytical skills, as they gather evidence to support their stance. Debating also improves public speaking abilities, as participants must articulate their thoughts clearly and persuasively. Additionally, debates promote critical thinking and logical reasoning, as individuals must challenge and defend their ideas.

Both group discussions and debates offer an opportunity for personal growth and self-reflection. They allow individuals to confront their own biases and preconceived notions, encouraging them to question their beliefs and expand their understanding of the world. By engaging in constructive dialogue, students and everyone can broaden their horizons and develop a well-rounded perspective on various issues.

To maximize the benefits of group discussions and debates, it is essential to create a supportive and inclusive environment. Facilitators should encourage active participation from all individuals, ensuring that everyone's voice is heard and respected. It is important to foster a culture of constructive criticism, where individuals can challenge ideas without personal attacks. By doing so, participants can learn to communicate effectively, resolve conflicts peacefully, and appreciate the value of diverse opinions.

In conclusion, group discussions and debates play a vital role in value education and character development. They empower students and everyone to express their opinions, develop critical thinking skills, and cultivate empathy and open-mindedness. By engaging in these activities, individuals can build a strong foundation for personal growth and contribute to a harmonious society.

Case Studies and Real-Life Examples

In the fascinating journey of character development, real-life examples and case studies play a pivotal role in illustrating the importance of value education. By examining the experiences of individuals from diverse backgrounds, we can gain valuable insights into the impact of values on personal growth and societal well-being. This subchapter delves into the realm of case studies and real-life examples, shedding light on the transformative power of value education.

One inspiring case study revolves around the life of Sarah, a young woman who grew up in a disadvantaged neighborhood. Despite facing numerous challenges, Sarah managed to rise above her circumstances and excel in her academics. How did she accomplish this? The answer lies in the strong foundation of values instilled in her by her parents and teachers. By emphasizing the importance of hard work, perseverance, and integrity, Sarah's mentors equipped her with the tools necessary to overcome adversity and achieve her goals.

Another compelling example pertains to the impact of value education on a community level. In a small town plagued by racial tension, a group of dedicated individuals initiated a value-based education program in local schools. Through workshops and interactive sessions, students were encouraged to embrace values such as empathy, respect, and tolerance. Over time, these efforts fostered a sense of unity and harmony within the community, breaking down barriers and creating an inclusive environment for all.

These case studies highlight the significance of value education in shaping individuals and communities. They demonstrate that values are not merely abstract concepts but powerful guiding principles that can empower individuals to overcome obstacles, make ethical choices, and contribute positively to society.

For students, these real-life examples serve as powerful motivation and inspiration. They provide concrete evidence that value education is not just a theoretical concept but an essential aspect of personal and academic success. By immersing themselves in these case studies, students can witness the transformative effects of values in the lives of real people, instilling in them a sense of purpose and a desire to embrace and embody these values themselves.

Beyond students, these examples are relevant to everyone. They remind us of the importance of value education in cultivating a strong foundation of character. Whether we are parents, educators, or members of society, we all have a responsibility to promote and prioritize value education. By doing so, we can contribute to the growth and development of individuals and communities, fostering a harmonious and prosperous society for all.

In conclusion, case studies and real-life examples provide concrete evidence of the transformative power of value education. They show us that values are not just theoretical concepts but practical tools that can shape individuals and communities. By embracing these examples, students and everyone can understand the importance of value education and its profound impact on personal growth and societal well-being. Let us embark on this journey together, building a strong foundation through the power of value education.

Service-Learning Projects

In today's fast-paced and competitive world, it is easy to get caught up in the pursuit of individual success and material possessions. However, it is important to remember that true happiness and fulfillment come from something more meaningful – making a positive impact on the lives of others. This is where service-learning projects play a crucial role in shaping our character and instilling the values that are essential for our personal and collective growth.

Service-learning projects provide students with a unique opportunity to apply their knowledge and skills in a real-world setting while addressing important social issues. By actively engaging in these projects, students not only gain a deeper understanding of the challenges faced by their communities but also develop a sense of empathy and compassion. This hands-on experience allows them to witness the power of their actions and discover the joy that comes from helping others.

One of the key benefits of service-learning projects is the development of valuable life skills. As students work collaboratively with their peers and community members, they learn the importance of effective communication, teamwork, and problem-solving. These skills are not only crucial for their academic and professional success but also for building strong relationships and becoming responsible citizens.

Furthermore, service-learning projects contribute to the development of a strong moral compass. By actively engaging in activities that promote social justice, equality, and environmental sustainability, students learn to prioritize the common good over personal gain. This understanding of ethical principles and values forms the foundation of a strong character, guiding students to make choices that positively impact their communities and the world at large.

Service-learning projects are not only beneficial for students but also for everyone involved. Communities benefit from the contributions made by these projects, whether it be through environmental conservation, literacy programs, or support for marginalized groups. These projects create a sense of unity and solidarity, fostering a culture of compassion and social responsibility.

In conclusion, service-learning projects are of utmost importance in value education and character development. They provide students with the opportunity to learn, grow, and contribute to their communities. By engaging in these projects, students develop essential life skills, deepen their understanding of social issues, and cultivate a strong moral compass. Ultimately, service-learning projects empower individuals to become agents of positive change and create a more just and compassionate society.

Reflection and Self-Assessment

In the journey of personal growth and character development, reflection and self-assessment play a crucial role. These practices enable individuals to gain a deeper understanding of themselves, their values, and their actions. In this subchapter, we will explore the significance of reflection and self-assessment in building a strong foundation through value education.

Reflection is the process of introspection, where one carefully examines their thoughts, feelings, and experiences. It allows individuals to delve into their actions, their motivations, and their impact on others. By taking the time to reflect, students and individuals can identify their strengths and areas for improvement, making it a valuable tool for personal growth.

Self-assessment, on the other hand, involves evaluating one's own performance and progress. It requires individuals to critically analyze their actions and measure them against their values and goals. Self-assessment helps students identify their strengths, weaknesses, and areas where they need to put in more effort. It fosters self-awareness and self-improvement.

Both reflection and self-assessment are essential components of value education. They enable students and individuals to align their actions with their values and develop a strong moral compass. Through reflection, students can understand the impact of their actions on themselves and others, fostering empathy and compassion. Self-assessment helps them identify areas where they can improve their character and make positive changes in their behavior.

In addition to personal growth, reflection and self-assessment also contribute to academic success. By reflecting on their learning experiences, students can identify effective study strategies, areas where they struggle, and seek assistance when needed. Self-assessment allows students to take ownership of their education and set realistic goals to achieve academic excellence.

Moreover, reflection and self-assessment are lifelong skills that extend beyond the classroom. In all aspects of life, individuals can benefit from taking the time to reflect on their actions and assess their progress. It allows them to continuously grow, adapt, and make meaningful contributions to society.

In conclusion, reflection and self-assessment are integral to the impotent of value education. By engaging in these practices, students and individuals can develop a strong foundation, align their actions with their values, and foster personal and academic growth. It is through reflection and self-assessment that we can build a better future for ourselves and others.

Chapter 5: Assessing Character Development through Value Education

Evaluating Character Traits

In this subchapter, we will explore the importance of evaluating character traits in building a strong foundation for personal and societal growth. Character development is an integral part of value education, and it plays a crucial role in shaping individuals' lives. Whether you are a student or anyone interested in personal development, understanding and evaluating character traits is essential.

Character traits are the qualities and attributes that make up an individual's personality and define who they are. These traits include values such as honesty, integrity, empathy, resilience, and responsibility, among others. Evaluating these traits allows us to assess our strengths and weaknesses, enabling us to work towards personal growth and self-improvement.

The evaluation process begins with self-reflection and introspection. Students and individuals are encouraged to examine their behavior, thoughts, and actions to identify their character strengths and areas that require improvement. This introspective approach helps in developing self-awareness and understanding one's moral compass.

Evaluating character traits also involves seeking feedback from others. This feedback can come from teachers, mentors, peers, and family members who have observed our behavior and interactions. Honest feedback helps us gain a different perspective and identify blind spots that we may not be aware of. It provides an opportunity to recognize areas where we excel and those that need attention.

Furthermore, evaluating character traits involves setting goals for personal growth. Once we have identified our strengths and weaknesses, we can establish specific objectives to enhance our positive traits and work on areas that need improvement. These goals act as a roadmap for character development, allowing us to track our progress and make necessary adjustments along the way.

It is important to remember that character development is a lifelong journey. Evaluating character traits is not a one-time process but rather a continuous effort. As we grow and face new experiences, our character traits evolve, and it is crucial to regularly assess and adapt them accordingly.

By actively evaluating character traits, students and individuals can build a strong foundation for personal and societal growth. It enhances self-awareness, cultivates positive values, and promotes ethical decision-making. Ultimately, embracing the importance of evaluating character traits leads to a more compassionate, responsible, and successful individual, positively impacting both personal and professional aspects of life.

So, let us embark on this journey of self-reflection and evaluation, for it is through understanding and improving our character traits that we can truly build a strong foundation for a fulfilling and purposeful life.

Self-Reflection and Self-Assessment Tools

In today's fast-paced and ever-changing world, it is essential for individuals to constantly evaluate and improve themselves. Self-reflection and self-assessment tools play a crucial role in this process, enabling us to gain a deeper understanding of our values, beliefs, and character traits. In the book "Building a Strong Foundation: The Power of Value Education in Character Development," we delve into the importance of self-reflection and provide valuable tools to aid students and individuals in their personal growth journey.

Self-reflection is the act of examining one's thoughts, emotions, and actions. It allows us to gain insight into our strengths and weaknesses, enabling us to make positive changes. Through self-reflection, individuals can develop a greater sense of self-awareness, which is a fundamental aspect of personal growth. By understanding our values and beliefs, we can align our actions with our innermost principles, leading to a more fulfilling and purpose-driven life.

To facilitate self-reflection, this subchapter introduces various self-assessment tools. These tools are designed to help individuals evaluate different aspects of their lives, such as their values, goals, and personal development. Through exercises and activities, readers will be able to explore their core values, identify areas for improvement, and set goals that align with their values.

One of the self-assessment tools discussed in this subchapter is the values assessment exercise. By examining their values, readers will gain a deeper understanding of what truly matters to them. This exercise will guide individuals in identifying their core values and help them make decisions that are in alignment with these values. Additionally, readers will learn how to prioritize their values, ensuring that they dedicate their time and energy to what truly matters most to them.

Another self-assessment tool highlighted in this subchapter is the goal-setting exercise. Setting goals is an integral part of personal growth, as it provides direction and motivation. Through this exercise, readers will learn how to set realistic and achievable goals that are in alignment with their values. By reflecting on their goals regularly, individuals can track their progress and make necessary adjustments to stay on the path towards personal and academic success.

Ultimately, self-reflection and self-assessment tools are invaluable in nurturing a strong foundation in character development. By engaging in self-reflection and utilizing these tools, students and individuals will be able to make informed choices, develop their character traits, and lead a more purposeful and fulfilling life. This subchapter aims to empower readers by providing them with the necessary knowledge and tools to embark on their personal growth journey. Whether you are a student or anyone seeking personal development, the significance of value education cannot be overstated, and self-reflection is an essential component of this transformative process.

Feedback and Support for Continuous Growth

In the journey of personal growth and character development, feedback and support play a crucial role. In this subchapter, we will explore the significance of feedback and support in our lives, particularly in the context of value education. This chapter is addressed to students and everyone who recognizes the importance of value education in shaping their lives.

Feedback is a powerful tool that allows us to reflect on our actions, thoughts, and behaviors. It provides us with valuable insights into our strengths and areas for improvement. Without feedback, we may remain unaware of our blind spots and miss out on opportunities for growth. Therefore, it is essential to cultivate a mindset that welcomes and values feedback.

As students, feedback from teachers, mentors, and peers helps us understand our progress and areas where we can enhance our character. Constructive criticism allows us to develop self-awareness and make positive changes. By actively seeking feedback, we can gain a deeper understanding of ourselves and work towards continuous improvement.

Support is another crucial element in our journey of growth. It provides us with the encouragement and motivation to overcome challenges and pursue our goals. When we have a supportive community, we feel empowered to take risks, explore new horizons, and make positive choices.

Value education is of paramount importance in our lives. It equips us with the necessary tools to navigate through challenges, make ethical decisions, and lead a purposeful life. Feedback and support play a vital role in reinforcing the values we have learned. They help us internalize these values and translate them into our actions and relationships.

When we receive feedback that aligns with the values we hold dear, it reinforces our commitment to those values. Conversely, when we receive feedback that challenges our values, it allows us to reflect on our beliefs and make necessary adjustments. Support from our community further strengthens our convictions and helps us stay true to our values, even in the face of adversity.

In conclusion, feedback and support are integral parts of our journey towards continuous growth and character development. As students and individuals who recognize the importance of value education, we must actively seek feedback, embrace it with an open mind, and use it as a catalyst for positive change. Simultaneously, we must surround ourselves with a supportive community that nurtures our values and provides us with the encouragement to strive for personal and moral excellence. By leveraging feedback and support, we can build a strong foundation of values that will guide us throughout our lives.

Chapter 6: Addressing Challenges in Value Education

Overcoming Resistance to Change

Change is an inevitable part of life, yet it is often met with resistance. Whether it is a change in our personal lives or within the larger society, the fear of the unknown and the comfort of familiarity often hold us back. However, in order to grow and develop as individuals and as a society, it is essential to overcome this resistance to change.

In the context of education, change is crucial for progress. This is where the importance of value education comes into play. Value education helps us understand the significance of change and how it can shape our character and overall development. By instilling values such as adaptability, open-mindedness, and resilience, value education equips students with the tools to overcome resistance to change.

One of the primary reasons people resist change is the fear of the unknown. We tend to cling to what is familiar because it provides us with a sense of security and comfort. Value education helps us recognize and reframe this fear by teaching us to embrace new experiences and view change as an opportunity for growth. It encourages us to step out of our comfort zones and explore new possibilities, ultimately broadening our horizons.

Another reason for resistance to change is the fear of failure. Change often brings uncertainty, and with uncertainty comes the possibility of making mistakes. However, value education teaches us that failure is not the end but rather a stepping stone towards success. It emphasizes the importance of learning from our mistakes and using them as a catalyst for personal growth. By embracing this mindset, we can overcome the fear of failure and navigate through change with confidence and resilience.

Moreover, value education fosters open-mindedness and empathy, enabling us to see change from different perspectives. It encourages us to listen to others, respect their opinions, and consider alternative viewpoints. Through this process, we develop a broader understanding of change and its potential benefits. Value education also emphasizes the importance of teamwork and collaboration, as working together can make adapting to change easier and more effective.

In conclusion, overcoming resistance to change is essential for personal and societal growth. Value education plays a crucial role in helping students and individuals understand the impotence of change and develop the necessary skills to embrace it. By nurturing adaptability, open-mindedness, and resilience, value education equips us to overcome the fear of the unknown and the comfort of familiarity. It empowers us to view change as an opportunity for growth rather than a threat, ultimately paving the way for a stronger, more resilient society.

Dealing with Diverse Value Systems

In today's interconnected world, it is essential to recognize and respect the existence of diverse value systems. As students and individuals, we encounter people from various backgrounds, cultures, and beliefs on a daily basis. Understanding and appreciating these differences can lead to a more harmonious and inclusive society. This subchapter aims to shed light on the importance of value education in handling these diverse value systems.

Value education plays a pivotal role in shaping our character and developing a strong foundation. It teaches us to embrace diversity and to respect the beliefs and values of others. By promoting empathy, tolerance, and open-mindedness, value education enables us to navigate the complexities of a multicultural world.

One of the key aspects of dealing with diverse value systems is recognizing that no single value system is superior to another. Each person's beliefs and values are shaped by their culture, upbringing, and personal experiences. By acknowledging this, we can foster a sense of equality and fairness, promoting a society where all individuals are valued and respected.

Moreover, value education equips us with the necessary skills to engage in constructive dialogues. It teaches us to listen actively, to consider different perspectives, and to communicate effectively. By engaging in respectful conversations, we can bridge gaps, build connections, and create a sense of unity.

Dealing with diverse value systems also calls for personal reflection and introspection. It prompts us to examine our own values, biases, and prejudices. By understanding ourselves better, we become more accepting and compassionate towards others. Value education encourages self-awareness and helps us challenge our preconceived notions, allowing for personal growth and development.

In a world where conflicts and misunderstandings often arise due to differences in values, value education becomes even more imperative. It provides us with the tools to resolve conflicts peacefully and to find common ground. By promoting dialogue, understanding, and compromise, we can build bridges and foster a more inclusive society.

In conclusion, understanding and dealing with diverse value systems is crucial for students and individuals alike. Value education equips us with the skills and mindset necessary to navigate a multicultural world. By promoting empathy, tolerance, and open-mindedness, we can build a strong foundation for character development and create a more harmonious and inclusive society.

Handling Ethical Dilemmas

In our journey through life, we often come across situations that challenge our moral compass. These moments, known as ethical dilemmas, force us to make difficult decisions that may have significant consequences. How we navigate these dilemmas says a lot about our character and the values we hold dear.

Understanding the importance of value education in character development is crucial for students and everyone alike. Building a strong foundation in ethical decision-making is not only essential for personal growth but also for creating a harmonious society. This subchapter delves into the intricacies of handling ethical dilemmas, providing valuable insights and practical strategies to confront these challenges head-on.

Ethical dilemmas can arise in various aspects of our lives, from personal relationships to professional environments. The decisions we make in these situations can have lasting effects on our well-being and the well-being of those around us. That is why it is crucial to cultivate a strong sense of ethics and moral values.

One effective approach to handling ethical dilemmas is to start with self-reflection. Examining our personal values and beliefs allows us to identify the principles that guide our moral compass. By gaining clarity on our values, we can better understand what is truly important to us and make decisions that align with our principles.

Another helpful strategy is seeking guidance from trusted mentors or role models who have faced similar ethical dilemmas. Learning from their experiences can provide valuable insights and alternative perspectives, helping us make more informed decisions. Additionally, engaging in dialogue with peers or professionals from different fields can broaden our understanding of ethical issues and challenge our preconceived notions.

When confronted with an ethical dilemma, it is essential to consider the potential consequences of each possible course of action. Weighing the short-term benefits against the long-term effects is critical to ensure the decisions we make are not only morally sound but also beneficial to ourselves and society at large.

Furthermore, maintaining open communication and transparency is vital when dealing with ethical dilemmas. By discussing the issue with those involved, we can foster understanding, empathy, and cooperation, leading to a resolution that upholds ethical principles while minimizing harm.

Ultimately, handling ethical dilemmas requires a combination of self-awareness, empathy, critical thinking, and a commitment to upholding moral values. By incorporating these skills into our decision-making process, we can navigate the complexities of ethical dilemmas with integrity and contribute to the creation of a more ethical and compassionate world. Remember, each ethical dilemma we face is an opportunity for growth and the strengthening of our character.

Chapter 7: The Role of Value Education in Building a Strong Society

Building Ethical Leaders

Ethics and moral values play a crucial role in shaping individuals into responsible and compassionate leaders. In today's fast-paced world, it is more important than ever to focus on value education and character development. This subchapter, titled "Building Ethical Leaders," aims to highlight the significance of instilling strong ethical values in students and everyone alike.

In our society, where success is often equated with material wealth and personal gain, the importance of ethical leadership cannot be underestimated. Ethical leaders are those who are guided by a strong moral compass, making decisions that prioritize the greater good over personal interests. They are individuals who understand the significance of integrity, honesty, empathy, and accountability.

As students, you are the future leaders of our world, and it is crucial to recognize the power and impact you can have in creating positive change. By focusing on value education and character development, you will be equipped with the necessary tools to become ethical leaders who can navigate complex challenges with integrity and compassion.

Value education is not limited to the classroom; it extends to every aspect of life. It is about embracing and implementing core ethical values such as respect, honesty, responsibility, fairness, and empathy in all interactions. These values serve as a foundation for building strong character, fostering meaningful relationships, and making ethical decisions.

By building ethical leaders, we create a ripple effect that transcends generations. Ethical leaders inspire others to follow their example, creating a culture of integrity and compassion. They prioritize the well-being of others, champion social justice causes, and work towards a more inclusive and sustainable future.

In today's rapidly changing world, where ethical dilemmas are abundant, the need for ethical leaders is more important than ever. Whether it's in the corporate world, politics, healthcare, or any other field, ethical leaders are the driving force behind positive change. They have the ability to influence and shape society, leaving a lasting impact on future generations.

In conclusion, this subchapter emphasizes the importance of value education and character development in building ethical leaders. As students and individuals, it is our responsibility to cultivate strong ethical values, prioritize the greater good, and lead with integrity. By doing so, we contribute to a better future, one where ethical leadership is celebrated and revered.

Promoting Social Responsibility

In today's rapidly changing world, it is becoming increasingly important to recognize the significance of social responsibility. As students and members of society, we have a crucial role to play in shaping the future and creating a better world for ourselves and future generations. This subchapter aims to highlight the importance of promoting social responsibility and the role of value education in character development.

Social responsibility refers to the ethical obligation that each individual has to act in a way that benefits society as a whole. It encompasses a wide range of actions and behaviors, from being environmentally conscious to promoting equality and justice. By actively engaging in social responsibility, we can contribute to the betterment of our communities and make a positive impact on the world around us.

Value education plays a vital role in fostering social responsibility. It equips individuals with the necessary knowledge, skills, and values to become responsible citizens. Through value education, students learn about the importance of compassion, empathy, and respect for others. They are encouraged to think critically, challenge societal norms, and take action to address social issues.

By promoting social responsibility, we can create a society that values inclusivity and diversity. Through collaborative efforts, we can work towards breaking down barriers and eliminating discrimination. Students can actively participate in volunteer activities, community service, or advocacy campaigns to address various social issues such as poverty, gender inequality, climate change, and more.

Moreover, promoting social responsibility also helps in developing essential life skills. By engaging in activities that promote social responsibility, students can enhance their communication skills, teamwork abilities, and problem-solving capabilities. These skills are not only beneficial for their personal growth but also highly valued by employers in the professional world.

In conclusion, promoting social responsibility is of utmost importance for students and everyone in society. As we recognize the importance of value education in character development, we understand that it provides the foundation for instilling social responsibility in individuals. By actively engaging in social responsibility, we can create a better world for ourselves and future generations, where everyone is treated with dignity and respect, and where equality and justice prevail. Let us embark on this journey together and build a strong foundation for a brighter future.

Fostering Inclusive and Harmonious Communities

In today's diverse and interconnected world, the importance of fostering inclusive and harmonious communities cannot be overstated. As students and individuals, we have a crucial role to play in creating an environment where everyone feels valued, respected, and included. This subchapter delves into the significance of value education in character development, specifically focusing on the immense impact it can have on building strong and inclusive communities.

Value education serves as a powerful tool for nurturing empathy, understanding, and compassion among individuals. By instilling core values such as respect, tolerance, and acceptance, it empowers us to embrace diversity and promote harmonious coexistence. When we recognize and appreciate the unique perspectives, cultures, and backgrounds of those around us, we pave the way for a truly inclusive society.

One of the key aspects of value education is developing a sense of social responsibility. As students, we are not just learners; we are also members of our communities. By actively participating in community service initiatives, volunteering, and engaging in acts of kindness, we contribute to the betterment of society and foster a sense of unity. These actions not only benefit others but also provide us with valuable opportunities for personal growth and character development.

Additionally, value education equips us with the necessary skills to navigate conflicts and address societal challenges in a peaceful and constructive manner. It teaches us the importance of effective communication, active listening, and finding common ground. By cultivating these skills, we learn to resolve differences amicably, promote dialogue, and work towards sustainable solutions that benefit everyone involved.

Furthermore, value education encourages us to challenge stereotypes and prejudices, promoting a more inclusive and egalitarian society. By examining our own biases and questioning societal norms, we become agents of change, breaking down barriers and promoting social justice. This process not only benefits marginalized communities but also enriches our own lives by broadening our perspectives and deepening our understanding of the world.

In conclusion, the importance of value education in fostering inclusive and harmonious communities cannot be emphasized enough. By instilling core values, developing a sense of social responsibility, and equipping individuals with conflict resolution skills, value education enables us to create a world where every individual is valued and respected. As students and members of society, it is our responsibility to embrace the power of value education and actively contribute to building strong, inclusive, and harmonious communities.

Chapter 8: The Long-Term Impact of Value Education on Students

Enhancing Emotional Intelligence and Interpersonal Skills

In today's fast-paced and interconnected world, the ability to understand and manage our emotions, as well as effectively interact with others, has become more crucial than ever. This subchapter aims to explore the significance of enhancing emotional intelligence and interpersonal skills in the context of value education, and how it contributes to building a strong foundation for character development.

Emotional intelligence refers to the capacity to recognize, understand, and manage our own emotions, as well as empathize with others. It plays a vital role in shaping our relationships, decision-making, and overall well-being. By enhancing emotional intelligence, students can cultivate self-awareness, self-regulation, motivation, empathy, and social skills, which are all fundamental aspects of personal and interpersonal growth.

Value education acts as a guiding force in nurturing emotional intelligence and interpersonal skills. It provides a framework to help students identify and align their values with their actions, fostering integrity, empathy, respect, and responsibility. Through value education, students learn to navigate through challenging situations, resolve conflicts, and communicate effectively, promoting healthy relationships and a positive social environment.

One of the key reasons why emotional intelligence and interpersonal skills are essential is their impact on mental health. Students who possess emotional intelligence can better manage stress, anxiety, and other psychological challenges. They are more likely to develop coping mechanisms, seek support when needed, and maintain a balanced mental well-being. Furthermore, strong interpersonal skills enable students to build and sustain meaningful relationships, fostering a sense of belonging and support systems.

In addition to personal growth, enhancing emotional intelligence and interpersonal skills also has broader societal implications. Students who excel in these areas are more likely to become empathetic and compassionate citizens, contributing positively to their communities. They possess the skills to collaborate, resolve conflicts peacefully, and embrace diversity, which are all vital in creating inclusive and harmonious societies.

In conclusion, the importance of enhancing emotional intelligence and interpersonal skills cannot be overstated. Through value education, students can develop these crucial abilities that are essential for their personal growth, mental well-being, and contribution to society. By investing in value education, we are building a strong foundation for character development, empowering students to face the challenges of the world with integrity, empathy, and resilience.

Developing a Strong Moral Compass

In today's fast-paced and complex world, it is more important than ever to cultivate a strong moral compass. This subchapter aims to shed light on the significance of value education and its role in character development, addressing students and everyone who recognizes the importance of this topic.

Value education is the process of imparting moral values, ethical principles, and character traits to individuals. It equips us with the necessary tools to navigate the challenges of life while making informed decisions that align with our personal and societal values. By developing a strong moral compass, we gain a sense of direction and purpose, enabling us to lead meaningful and fulfilling lives.

The importance of value education cannot be overstated. It serves as a guidepost in our daily decision-making, helping us distinguish right from wrong. It instills qualities such as honesty, integrity, empathy, and respect, fostering a positive and inclusive environment. Moreover, value education empowers individuals to overcome obstacles, develop resilience, and contribute positively to society.

For students, value education is particularly crucial as it shapes their character during their formative years. It provides a solid foundation upon which they can build their lives and make informed choices. By inculcating values early on, students develop a moral compass that will guide them throughout their personal and professional journeys.

Value education also has broader societal implications. In a world where confusion, moral dilemmas, and ethical challenges abound, a strong moral compass can help individuals resist negative influences, such as peer pressure or societal expectations. By making value education a priority, we foster a society that is not only morally upright but also compassionate, just, and responsible.

To develop a strong moral compass, one must engage in self-reflection, introspection, and critical thinking. It involves questioning our beliefs, examining our actions, and aligning them with our core values. It requires us to be open-minded, receptive to diverse perspectives, and willing to learn from our mistakes.

In conclusion, value education plays a pivotal role in developing a strong moral compass. It equips individuals, especially students, with the tools and principles needed to navigate life's challenges with integrity and grace. By prioritizing value education, we can build a society that upholds ethical values, fosters personal growth, and contributes positively to the betterment of humanity.

Nurturing Ethical Decision-Making Skills

In today's fast-paced and ever-changing world, it is becoming increasingly important for individuals to possess strong ethical decision-making skills. These skills not only shape our character but also have a profound impact on our personal and professional lives. In this subchapter, we will explore the significance of nurturing ethical decision-making skills and the role of value education in character development.

Ethical decision-making skills are the foundation of a healthy and productive society. They enable individuals to make choices that are morally right and aligned with their values. By developing these skills, students and everyone can navigate through complex situations and dilemmas with integrity and empathy. Ethical decision-making requires critical thinking, reflection, and the ability to consider the consequences of our actions on others.

Value education plays a pivotal role in fostering ethical decision-making skills. It provides individuals with a framework to understand and evaluate ethical dilemmas based on principles such as honesty, respect, fairness, and responsibility. Through value education, students and everyone can develop a moral compass that guides their actions and choices. It equips them with the tools to analyze situations from different perspectives and make informed decisions that promote the greater good.

The importance of value education in character development cannot be overstated. It nurtures qualities such as empathy, compassion, and integrity, which are essential for building strong and meaningful relationships. Furthermore, value education instills a sense of social responsibility and encourages individuals to become active contributors to their communities. By integrating ethical decision-making skills into their daily lives, students and everyone can become agents of positive change in society.

In conclusion, nurturing ethical decision-making skills is of utmost importance in today's world. Value education plays a crucial role in developing these skills and shaping our character. By understanding the significance of ethical decision-making and embracing value education, students and everyone can cultivate a strong foundation for personal growth and contribute to a more ethical and compassionate society.

Chapter 9: Value Education Beyond the Classroom

Community Engagement and Volunteerism

In today's fast-paced and self-centered world, it is crucial for students and everyone to understand the importance of community engagement and volunteerism. This subchapter explores the power of value education in character development, emphasizing the significance of giving back to society.

Community engagement refers to actively participating in activities that benefit the local community. It involves collaborating with others to address social issues and create a positive impact. By engaging with the community, students and individuals can develop a deeper understanding of the challenges people face and the various ways they can contribute to making a difference.

Volunteerism, on the other hand, involves offering one's time, skills, and resources to support a cause or organization without expecting any compensation. It is a powerful tool for personal growth, as it allows individuals to develop empathy, compassion, and a sense of responsibility towards others. Engaging in volunteer work not only benefits the community but also helps individuals cultivate essential life skills and values.

Value education plays a crucial role in character development, as it instills a sense of morality, ethics, and empathy in individuals. By integrating value education into their lives, students and individuals become more aware of their roles and responsibilities within their communities. They learn to appreciate the importance of helping others and actively seek opportunities to contribute positively.

Community engagement and volunteerism offer a wide range of benefits to students and everyone involved. Firstly, it promotes personal growth and self-esteem. When individuals witness the positive impact they can make on others' lives, they gain a sense of purpose and fulfillment. Secondly, it enhances social and communication skills. Engaging with diverse groups of people fosters understanding, tolerance, and effective communication. Lastly, it broadens perspectives and creates a sense of global citizenship. By actively participating in community activities, individuals become aware of global issues, promoting a more inclusive and compassionate society.

In conclusion, community engagement and volunteerism are vital components of character development and value education. By actively participating in these activities, students and individuals not only contribute to the betterment of society but also develop essential life skills and values. Embracing the power of community engagement and volunteerism allows us to build a strong foundation for a more empathetic, responsible, and compassionate future.

Applying Values in Real-Life Situations

In today's fast-paced and ever-changing world, it has become increasingly important to equip ourselves with the necessary tools to navigate through life's challenges. While academic knowledge is undoubtedly crucial, it is equally essential to understand the significance of values and their application in real-life situations. This subchapter aims to shed light on the importance of value education and how it can shape our character development.

Values serve as guiding principles that shape our thoughts, actions, and decisions. They provide us with a moral compass, allowing us to distinguish right from wrong, and make choices that align with our beliefs. However, merely knowing about values is not enough; it is the application of these values in various contexts that truly brings about a positive impact.

Real-life situations often pose dilemmas where individuals are faced with conflicting interests or ethical decisions. It is during these moments that the application of values becomes paramount. For example, in a situation where honesty is tested, a person who has imbibed the value of truthfulness will be more likely to choose the path of integrity, even if it means facing consequences. Similarly, individuals who possess empathy as a core value will be more inclined to understand and support others during times of crisis, fostering a sense of community and cooperation.

Value education also plays a vital role in fostering positive relationships. In our interactions with family, friends, and colleagues, the values we uphold greatly influence how we treat others. Respect, for instance, enables us to appreciate diversity and treat others with dignity. By applying respect in our daily lives, we can build harmonious relationships and contribute to a more inclusive society.

Moreover, value education empowers individuals to become responsible citizens. Values such as integrity, justice, and compassion guide us in making decisions that consider the well-being of others and the environment. By applying these values, we can contribute to sustainable development, social justice, and the preservation of our planet for future generations.

In conclusion, value education is of utmost importance for students and everyone alike. It goes beyond theoretical knowledge, urging us to apply values in real-life situations. By doing so, we develop strong character traits, make ethical choices, build meaningful relationships, and become responsible citizens. Let us embrace the power of value education and pave the way for a brighter and more compassionate future.

Creating a Lasting Legacy

In this subchapter, we delve into the importance of value education and its role in character development. This chapter is dedicated to students and everyone who recognizes the significance of building a strong foundation for a successful and fulfilling life.

Value education plays a pivotal role in shaping individuals into responsible and ethical citizens. It provides a framework for understanding the fundamental principles and values that guide our actions and decisions. By instilling these values, we lay the groundwork for personal growth, social harmony, and a lasting legacy.

At the core of value education is the belief that each person possesses innate worth and dignity. It is through the exploration and cultivation of values such as respect, empathy, integrity, and compassion that we develop strong character traits. These values not only benefit us individually but also contribute to a more harmonious and inclusive society.

By embracing the importance of value education, students can build a solid foundation upon which to navigate life's challenges with integrity and purpose. It provides them with a moral compass, guiding their decisions and actions towards positive outcomes. When faced with dilemmas or difficult choices, individuals grounded in value education can rely on their principles to make wise and ethical decisions.

Moreover, value education empowers students to become agents of change in their communities. Through understanding the significance of values such as social responsibility, justice, and equality, they are equipped to address societal issues and contribute positively to the world around them. By nurturing a sense of empathy and compassion, students can create a lasting legacy by making a difference in the lives of others.

In today's fast-paced and ever-changing world, the importance of value education cannot be overstated. As technology advances and globalization accelerates, it is crucial to ensure that individuals possess a strong moral foundation. Value education provides the tools and knowledge necessary to navigate the complexities of the modern world while staying grounded in timeless principles.

In conclusion, value education is of paramount importance for students and everyone. It serves as a guiding light, enabling individuals to develop strong character traits, make ethical decisions, and contribute positively to society. By embracing value education, we lay the foundation for a lasting legacy that transcends time and impacts future generations. Let us embark on this journey together, for the betterment of ourselves and the world we inhabit.

Chapter 10: Conclusion and Future of Value Education

Recap of Key Learnings

In this subchapter, we will recapitulate the essential lessons we have learned throughout this book on "Building a Strong Foundation: The Power of Value Education in Character Development." Whether you are a student or someone interested in the importance of value education, this recap will serve as a valuable reminder of the key takeaways.

Throughout this book, we have emphasized the importance of value education and its role in shaping our character development. Value education goes beyond academic knowledge; it focuses on instilling moral values, ethics, and compassion in individuals. These values form the basis of our interactions with others and contribute to creating a harmonious society.

One of the key learnings from this book is the understanding that value education is not limited to classrooms or academic institutions. It is a lifelong process that starts at home and continues throughout our lives. We have explored various ways to incorporate value education into our daily lives, such as practicing gratitude, empathy, and kindness towards others.

Another crucial aspect highlighted in this book is the role of role models in value education. We have discussed the significance of having positive role models who embody the values we aspire to acquire. By observing and learning from these individuals, we can develop a strong foundation of values that will guide our actions and decisions.

Furthermore, we have explored the importance of self-reflection in value education. Taking the time to reflect on our actions, thoughts, and emotions allows us to identify areas for improvement and make necessary changes. It is through self-reflection that we can align our behavior with our values and lead a more purposeful life.

Additionally, this book has emphasized the significance of empathy and understanding in value education. By placing ourselves in others' shoes and seeking to understand their perspectives, we can foster a sense of unity and compassion. This enables us to build stronger relationships and contribute positively to our communities.

In conclusion, this subchapter has provided a brief overview of the key learnings from "Building a Strong Foundation: The Power of Value Education in Character Development." As students and individuals interested in the importance of value education, it is crucial to remember that value education is a lifelong journey that starts with ourselves and extends to those around us. By embodying moral values, learning from positive role models, practicing self-reflection, and cultivating empathy, we can build a strong foundation of character that will positively impact our lives and society as a whole.

Embracing Value Education for a Better Future

Value education plays a crucial role in shaping the character of individuals and ultimately, the future of society as a whole. In today's fast-paced and competitive world, it is essential for students and everyone to recognize the importance of value education and its impact on personal growth and development. This subchapter aims to shed light on the significance of value education and how it can pave the way for a better future.

Value education encompasses a wide range of principles and virtues that guide individuals in making ethical and responsible choices. It instills moral values such as honesty, integrity, empathy, respect, and compassion, which are fundamental for building strong character. These values act as a compass, helping individuals navigate through the complexities of life and make decisions that positively impact not only themselves but also those around them.

For students, value education serves as a solid foundation for their academic and personal growth. It equips them with the necessary tools to face challenges, overcome obstacles, and make informed decisions. By embracing value education, students develop a strong sense of self-awareness, self-discipline, and self-confidence, which are vital attributes for success in any endeavor.

Beyond the individual level, value education has a far-reaching impact on society. When individuals internalize and practice values such as respect for diversity, social responsibility, and environmental consciousness, they contribute to the creation of a harmonious and inclusive community. Value education fosters a culture of empathy and understanding, promoting tolerance and acceptance among people from different backgrounds and beliefs.

Moreover, the importance of value education extends to ensuring a sustainable future for our planet. By instilling values of environmental stewardship and sustainable living, individuals become conscious of their ecological footprint and strive to protect and preserve the environment for future generations.

In conclusion, value education is of utmost importance for students and everyone. It provides the necessary foundation for character development, personal growth, and societal harmony. By embracing value education, individuals can shape a better future based on ethical principles, empathy, and responsible decision-making. Let us recognize the impotence of value education and actively incorporate its teachings into our lives, for it is through the power of values that we can build a strong foundation for a brighter tomorrow.

Printed in the USA
CPSIA information can be obtained
at www.ICGtesting.com
LVHW051216190424
777773LV00014B/704